అరుణాచలశివ

The Essence of the Spiritual Instruction

by

Bhagavan Sri Ramana Maharshi

Translated with Commentary
by Nome

Published by
Society of Abidance in Truth (SAT)
1834 Ocean Street
Santa Cruz, CA 95060 USA
(831) 425-7287
www.SATRamana.org / email: sat@cruzio.com

First Edition

Printed in India

Om Namo Bhagavate Sri Ramanaya

Revealing the Truth,
Removing all obstacles,
Bestowing Knowledge,
As the Lord of all the retinues, He abides.

Wielding undivided Knowledge,
Destroying a mountain of illusion,
Liberating all from delusion's dream,
As that which is excellent for the Realization of
Brahman, He shines.

Existing without another,
Granting to all the nectar of immortality,
Silencing all doubts forever,
As That which alone exists, Siva, He is.

* * *

Dakshinamurti being the beginning,
Sankara Acarya being in the middle,
Ramana Sadguru being the end,
To this lineage of Gurus, obeisance!

Acknowledgements

Deep appreciation and gratitude are here expressed for the proofreading efforts and suggestions of Ganesh Sadasivan, Sangeeta Raman, Raman Muthukrishnan, Sasvati, and Jim Clark. There is gratitude to Shashikanth Rao for so kindly reviewing the first half of the text and giving corrections and suggestions pertaining to it. Gratitude is also here expressed to Surekha Vinchurkar for very kindly reviewing the Sanskrit text and the English translation. There is appreciation for the assistance given by Seetharaman Mahadevan. Thank you, Sasvati, for the entire layout and design and thanks to Raman Muthukrishnan and Sasvati for the printing arrangements. Thankfulness is expressed here to Raman Muthukrishnan, Sangeeta Raman, and Myra Taylor for funding the printing of this book and to all who support the SAT temple and its endeavors. There is appreciation for all those who have preserved, previously translated, or disseminated this sacred text. Thank you, Omkarananda Ashram, for freely making available the Sanskrit font used in this book. Eternal gratitude and the heart's full devotion are to the divine source, Bhagavan Sri Ramana Maharshi.

Introduction

The Silent Instruction Manifests in Language

Bhagavan Sri Ramana Maharshi, abiding in the eternal Silence of the Self, composed *The Essence of Spiritual Instruction* for the supreme good of all in response to the supplications of the devoted Muruganar. The poet-devotee was writing in Tamil the story of the wayward rishis who dwelled in the Daruka forest and practiced rites for the attainment of powers that they desired. Their egos humbled by Siva and perceiving the error of their approach, they humbly sought spiritual instruction from Siva. Siva graciously bestowed the instruction, and it is these teachings that Muruganar requested Sri Bhagavan, Siva himself, to reveal in verse form. So, the Maharshi composed thirty verses in Tamil. The verses are contained in the first part of *Tiruvundiyar* as verses 103 through 132, which, in turn, is a song contained within *Sri Ramana Sannidhi Murai* as verses 1379 through 1408. These thirty verses are said to have been composed at one time during 1927 or shortly thereafter. Later, Sri Bhagavan translated them into Sanskrit. The Tamil version is entitled *Upadesa Undiyar*, and the Sanskrit version is entitled *Upadesa Sarah* (upadeśasāraḥ) and is also referred to as *Upadesa Saram.*

Translations and Commentaries

In the course of time, several English translations of these verses were published. Most of them include commentaries by the translators, or, at least, notes of explanation. Among these are the following, which are not intended as an exhaustive list but only what is at hand here:

The commentary of Sri A. R. Natarajan that accompanies his translation of the Sanskrit text into English, which is erudite, full of insightful wisdom, and permeated by his joyful devotion.

Upadesa Undiyar of Bhagavan Sri Ramana by Sri Sadhu Om and Michael James, translated from Tamil and published in 1986, which is very deep, precise, and informative, with an introduction and notes that emphasize the context and story in which the verses appear.

The English translations of Sri Sadhu Om from the Tamil text and Sri Viswanatha Swami from the Sanskrit text that appear in *The Works of Bhagavan Sri Ramana Maharshi in His Own Handwriting*.

The translation from Tamil with the commentary by B. V. Narasimhaswami in *Upadesa Saram* (1970 sixth edition).

The translation from Sanskrit, with a facsimile of the Maharshi's Sanskrit handwritten text, published as *Upadesa Sarah* by Sri Ramana Kshetra in Kerala in 1985.

The translation from Tamil by Sri R. Visvanathan and Sadhu Arunachala (A. W. Chadwick), entitled "Quintessence of Instruction" in *The Poems of Sri Ramana Maharshi*, published in 1960.

The translation from Sanskrit, with commentary, by Nagesh D. Sonde, published as *Upadesha Saram* in 1993.

The translation from Sanskrit, with commentary, by Shri Brahmananda Sarasvati, published as *Upadesha Saram* in 1993.

The translation from Sanskrit, with commentary, in *The Maharshi's Way* by D. M. Sastri, published in 1989.

The translation from Tamil and commentary by M. Anantanarayanan, published as *The Quintessence of Wisdom or the Thirty Verses of Sri Ramana* (1968 second edition).

The translation from Sanskrit, with commentary, by Swami Tejomayananda, published as *Upadesha Saar of Bhagwan Ramana Maharshi* in 1987.

The two different translations, both from Tamil, that appear in *Collected Works of Ramana Maharshi*, such as found in the third edition, 1968, by an unnamed translator and edited by Arthur Osborne and in the sixth edition, 1996, translated by Prof. K. Swaminathan. Both are entitled *The Essence of Instruction*.

In keeping with the story about Siva that forms the background of this set of thirty verses and the order in which they are placed, all of the commentaries treat this work as a terse yet sweeping overview of various spiritual practices, with the first half of the text dealing with these various practices and with teachings of Self-inquiry and Self-Knowledge being presented in the latter half.

Questions

Differences between the Tamil and Sanskrit versions of the text are apparent, and these may not be entirely attributable to mere differences in language. The differences may be assumed to be intentional and not accidental or incidental. As in the case of *Saddarsanam* (Sanskrit) and *Ulladu Narpadu* (Tamil), it is not at all reasonable to conceive that the Maharshi was in any manner unaware of these differences, which are changes that were made when the Sanskrit text was composed. Though it cannot now be determined with any certainty, it is possible that these changes represent insertion of further points or meaning or that they may represent refinement or enhancement of expression to bring forth nuances that may not be as sharply defined in the initial Tamil version. Of course, this cannot in any way lead to an inference that the Tamil text is lacking in any respect, for in it shines supreme wisdom, and it was written by the hand of Sri Ramana, Siva himself. Yet, this is also true of the Sanskrit text. So, why were these changes introduced by him?

The readily discernable facts are that the Tamil version was the initial one written about 1927, that the Sanskrit version was written later by Sri Bhagavan, that Sri Ramana used both in bestowing instruction, and that the differences, though slight, are not random or accidental.

Sri Bhagavan's use of the Sanskrit version when teaching is clearly evident. An example of this is found in *Talks with Sri Ramana Maharshi*, dialogue 222, July 2, 1936. Therein, he refers to the Sanskrit verses 10, 17, 19 directly and alludes to verses 21, 11, 13, 14, and perhaps others. He also refers to the text entirely or in part in *Talks with Sri Ramana Maharshi*, dialogue 376, March 21, 1937, dialogue 445, January 9, 1938, and dialogue 465, March 6, 1938. Were there reasons for his use of the Sanskrit text and Tamil text on different occasions?

All of the commentaries treat the verses as in an ascending order, and some explicitly state that their arrangement is so. This general trend in the text is easily perceived, yet a keen examination of some of the verses gives rise to the question as to whether this is entirely, consistently the case or not, such as with verses eight and nine preceding verse eleven.

If the verses are to be considered as in ascending order, why do the verses that give instruction in devotion (bhakti) not appear either immediately preceding or intermingled with those that pertain to inquiry (jnana, vicara)? In *Self-Realization* (pamphlet), he said, "There are only two ways to conquer destiny or to be independent of it," and "Complete effacement of the ego is necessary to conquer destiny, whether you achieve this effacement through Self-inquiry or through bhakti marga." In the light of such teaching, the presumption that these verses represent only a description of various paths in ascending order may become questionable. A further question arises as to why would incomplete methods be interspersed between complete ones.

"Upadesa" means spiritual instruction or teaching. Although the initial Tamil version calls these thirty verses *Upadesa Undiyar*, the latter word referring to a form of poetic meter, when the Sanskrit version was written, the title was changed to *Upadesa Sarah* (*Saram*) (upadeśasāraḥ), which means the essence of the spiritual instruction.Why entitle these verses "the essence" if the first half supposedly does not represent Bhagavan's own teachings? If the word "essence" was employed to mean a summary of the teachings given by Siva in ancient times, why did he not include the verses that set that context, as he did with the Tamil version? May the title also simultaneously carry another meaning pertaining purely to the essence, which is the Self, and the essential spiritual teaching, which is Self-Knowledge?

If the text was composed for Sri Ramana's disciples, devotees, and like-minded spiritual seekers, they were already familiar with, drawn to, and engaged in the spiritual practice of Self-inquiry. So, why would the first half deal with practices that they may have already transcended or which they would find as indirect in contrast to the inquiry? Certainly the creation of opinions by the spiritual aspirants about practices other than their own would not be advantageous for them, and Sri Bhagavan generally discouraged such concepts. Was it merely to declare the obvious fact that the most direct, or only actual, means for Self-Realization is Self-inquiry? ("To inquire, 'Who am I that am in bondage?' and thus know one's real nature is the only Liberation." *Self-Realization*, pamphlet) Even if this were the case, could there simultaneously be another purpose? The spiritual instruction bestowed by wondrous sages such as the Maharshi is all-comprehensive and simultaneously fulfills multiple spiritual purposes and benefits the seekers in a great many ways. Such is his Grace.

The Sanskrit version was recited daily before Sri Bhagavan as part of the Veda Parayana, and this practice of its recitation continues at Sri Ramanasramam to this day. Would it be extraordinary to suggest that the texts recited are relevant to his teachings? If they are relevant, do some of the verses that do not explicitly speak of Self-inquiry and Self-Knowledge carry an implicit meaning that is relevant to Self-inquiry and Self-Knowledge?

The Tamil text includes six introductory verses (Upodghatam), which very briefly summarize the context of the story in which the group of rishis requested spiritual instruction from Lord Siva, as well as five concluding verses of praise. When Sri Ramana composed the Sanskrit text, he did not include these but wrote just the thirty verses as a translation with, perhaps, some alterations. Even the word "undi-para" (leap and fly) that occurs in each verse of the Tamil version was not translated at all into the Sanskrit version. Such changes and the extraction of the instruction from the legendary context must have been for a purpose. Indeed, in his own handwriting of the Sanskrit, after the title and before the first verse of the text, he inserts "commences," to indicate the beginning of this text. May this represent more than a formality and be an actual indication of where one should start to understand this essence of the teaching? Similarly, in his own writing, the customary "concludes" ends the text, yet the word also means "complete." May this indicate that, deeply understood, these thirty verses form a complete instruction about that which is perfectly full?

An Approach in Self-Knowledge

In addition to the customary interpretation of the text, another approach to the Sanskrit version may be useful to discern the essence and what is to be derived from these verses by one who inquires in the one-pointed, ardent quest of nondual Self-Knowledge. Such an approach views all of the verses in the light of the Knowledge of the Self, the Reality, rather than as an exposition of a variety of practices. That is, it is an exposition of nonduality and Self-Knowledge from the very start and not only during the latter half of the text.

Thus, the entire text can be treated from the perspective of the essence and as an instruction about this essence, by the essence, to be realized by the essence, in the essence, as the essence. The essence is the Self and its Knowledge of itself. In this approach, the entirety of that which is declared by the Maharshi and all the implications thereof are directly applicable to one engaged in Self-inquiry and absorbed in Self-Knowledge.

This Commentary

Appending a commentary to a text may serve various and multiple purposes. Among these are:

an explanation of the words and phrases of the verses so that there is no misunderstanding concerning the terms employed;

an explanation of the basis of the verses, whether that be a description of the tradition or the revelation of the essential, spiritual, realized Knowledge, inclusive of how this is the continuous thread throughout a text;

the description of the results of practicing and realizing that which is stated in the verses, with explanations of the reasons why the results have such a connection;

and a demonstration of corresponding passages from scriptures and other sages, or even from the same sage, in order to clarify the meaning of those passages, clarify the meaning of the present verses, or show the continuation of, and correlation with, the timeless Truth that is expressed therein.

A commentary may also present doubts that could arise for the seeker accompanied by explanations that resolve such doubts to thereby reveal the verity, scope, and depth of the verse and the Knowledge expressed or implicit in it. These approaches are ultimately for the singular purpose of the realization of absolute Self-Knowledge within.

The ostensible meaning of the verses of *Upadesa Sarah* is plain and has already been thoroughly dealt with in other commentaries. Consequently, this is not emphasized here, and the approach taken in this commentary is different because of its specific focus. The emphasis is upon the profound significance of each verse for those already practicing Self-inquiry.

The approach presented in this commentary is the elucidation of both the basis and the results, or implications, of each verse. Each verse is treated in the light of Self-Knowledge, revealing that knowledge from which the verse comes forth, that is, the basis of declaring what the verse tersely proclaims, and, if this and the verse are comprehended, that which must necessarily be the case in light of such. In other words, the explanation is of why the content of the verse is stated, and, if one knows this reason, or basis, experientially and what is revealed by the verse, what one thus realizes. Thus, the focus is upon the root and the fruit.

The explanations are set forth as ten succinct, pithy points pertaining to each verse. The enumeration is for ease of reading and does not represent an ascending or descending order. Similarly, the points that may be considered the root and those that may be considered the fruit are freely mingled. All of the ten points refer to the verse they follow, each verse being considered distinct, as well as conjoined to the preceding or succeeding verses. The brevity of expression is intentional. If the meaning or the relevance to the verse is not immediately understood, meditation upon it in the form of inquiry to know oneself will yield the necessary clarity.

References to other works that contain records of Sri Bhagavan's teachings in order to demonstrate their correlation with the *Upadesa Sarah* verses and the commentary points, as well as references to other scriptural passages that expound the same teachings, have not been included in this commentary. Such references would have been too numerous; indeed, they could be a book in themselves.

Self-inquiry in the light of Sri Bhagavan's instruction will completely resolve any doubt so that abidance in the Self, as the Self, which is Self-Knowledge, unwaveringly remains.

This translation into English from Sanskrit is an attempt to provide a very literal translation, even to the extent of the preservation of the order of the words where feasible, similar to the approach taken in *Saddarsanam and An Inquiry into the Revelation of Truth and Oneself.* Alternative translations are provided for words and phrases in the notes immediately following each verse, and, in some cases, alternative translations for the entire verse are presented. In cases in which words that appear in the English translation are implied, but do not actually appear, in the Sanskrit text, this is indicated in the notes. The commentary includes the meaning of the alternative translations as well as the meaning selected for the primary translation. It is hoped that this manner of translation, along with the commentary, will help readers to dive deep into the sublime, profound teachings of Sri Bhagavan and thus realize the Self. An appendix that contains just the Sanskrit text with transliteration that incorporates the division of the words, except in instances of vowel sandhi, is included for ease of recitation and similar purposes.

Om Namo Bhagavate Sri Ramanaya

viṣaya prayojana sambandha adhikārin

(The subject, the aim, the relationship, and the person for whom the work is meant)

The Essence of the Spiritual Instruction graciously bestowed by Bhagavan Sri Ramana Maharshi as revealed in Self-Knowledge is that which is to be known. Abidance in the Self, as the Self, which is beyond all duality and of the nature of the highest Bliss, is the purpose. Being is Knowledge; so abidance in the Knowledge revealed is abidance as the real Being of the Self is the relation. Those who inquire to realize the Self are they for whom this is intended. They will comprehend.

श्री
उपदेशसारः ॥

śrī
upadeśasāraḥ ||

The Holy
Essence of the Spiritual Instruction

Note: The word for "holy" also means glorious, radiant.

प्रारभ्यते ॥

prārabhyate ||

Commences

कर्तुराज्ञया प्राप्यते फलम् ।
कर्म किं परं कर्म तज्जडम् ॥ १ ॥

karturājñayā prāpyate phalam |
karma kiṁ paraṁ karma tajjaḍam || 1 ||

By the command of the Creator the result is obtained.
Is karma the Supreme? That karma is inert. (1)

Note: "by the command" can be translated as from the command.
"By the command of the Creator" can be translated as by the direction of the doer.
"Doer" can be translated as maker.
"karma" means action.

Thus:

1. The means and the end are of the same nature.
2. Action cannot yield Self-Realization, which is the self-revelation of Para, the Absolute, the Supreme.
3. The Supreme Self's Knowledge of itself is Realization.
4. Knowledge is of the very nature of Consciousness.
5. Consciousness, Knowledge, can never be inert. Action is ever inert. Knowledge alone is the means to itself and is transcendent of the instruments of activity, which are the body, speech, and mind.
6. Destiny, the result of previous karma, is within the power of God perceived as a Creator and appears so long as the performer of action, or an individual to whom karma and destiny apply, is conceived.
7. Just as the individual performer of action does not exist as such, Creator-ship also is merely a conception, and their directions or commands are likewise. The Supreme Self is not inert, not affected by the inert, and possesses no qualities of the inert.
8. If one recognizes the inert nature of all action, he will remain unattached to all and will remain free of the superimposition of the inert upon himself.
9. The cause and the effect, the karma and the result, are the same and pertain to the inert. The Supreme is transcendent of causality.
10. The Supreme is real, revealed in divine, nonobjective Knowledge, which is the Knowledge of itself. The inert is non-Self and unreal. The unreal can neither produce nor determine the Real. The Realization of the Absolute Self can neither be produced by any activity, gross or subtle, nor be determined by such.

कृतिमहोदधौ पतनकारणम् ।
फलमशाश्वतं गतिनिरोधकम् ॥ २ ॥

kṛtimahodadhau patanakāraṇam ǀ
phalamaśāśvataṁ gatinirodhakam ǀǀ 2 ǀǀ

The non-eternal result, the cause of the falling into the great ocean of action,
Is the obstruction of progress. (2)

Note: "non-eternal" can be translated as transient.
"progress" can be translated as motion.

Thus:

1. Activity of any kind is transient, and the result of the non-eternal is only non-eternal and never otherwise.
2. The Self is eternal and is realized by the beginningless, endless light of innate Knowledge.
3. The eternal is Real, which ever is, and the non-eternal is unreal, which truly never is.
4. Non-eternality is indicative of the unreal but is not its definition.
5. A miniscule drop of illusion, assumed to be real, appears as an ocean into which the individual, who is the source of that drop and for whom it appears, misidentified as the experiencer and the performer of action, falls, just as one falls into a dream. Therein, one is buffeted by and submerged in karma.
6. Imagining the Self to be that which it is not, thc Real to be unreal and the unreal to be real, is the obstruction to spiritual progress, which is Liberation from the imagined bondage.
7. The result of the misidentification implicit in action performed in delusion and in the desire for the fruits of action is the same misidentification.
8. That result, with its cause and its further effects, is not eternal. One's own nature is eternal. Therefore, one is saved from drowning in samsara (illusory cycle of birth and death) and can proceed by true Self-Knowledge to realize the Ever-existent as such and as the Sole-existent.

9. Truly, the non-eternal is eternally not, and that goal to which the seeker of Liberation aspires is ever the case. Thus, progress is like awakening from a dream, in which one was drowning, to find repose in the place he ever actually was.
10. What is said of the Self, which is Being-Consciousness-Bliss, also pertains to Grace. By the Grace of Sri Bhagavan, we rise from the inert, as the living from the dead, the ocean of samsara completely evaporates, all obstructions vanish, and we abide in the eternal, as the eternal, by the light of His essential spiritual instruction.

ईश्वरार्पितं नेच्छया कृतम् ।
चित्तशोधकं मुक्तिसाधकम् ॥ ३ ॥

īśvarārpitaṁ necchayā kṛtam |
cittaśodhakaṁ muktisādhakam || 3 ||

Offered to the Lord, done not with desire,
It is a purifier of the mind, useful for Liberation. (3)

Note: "done not with desire" can be translated as done not according to desire.
"it" is implied.
"useful for" can be translated as a practice for, accomplishing.

Thus:

1. The Lord, the Supreme Self of all, is Bliss.
2. That happiness is alone desired in all desires.
3. The object associated with desire is inert. The essence of the desire is for the bliss, which is within.
4. One who knows this abandons desire, abides unattached, and is happy within.

5. The same thing that binds in ignorance becomes a means to, or an expression of, spiritual freedom in wisdom. Freedom is in the Lord. The experience of action changes from binding to liberating by offering.
6. That which is offered to the Lord does not bind, for it is not based upon misidentification and attachment.
7. An impure mind is one that believes its own imagination, in which the forms of misidentification and attachment are conceived and adhered to, which pursues happiness elsewhere, and which is confused due to its own extroversion. A pure mind, introspective and keenly discerning, loses its form and remains happily only as pure Consciousness.
8. Egoism is the veil. Offering all to the Lord, who is the Master without other, leaves no scope for the ego. Whatever diminishes the ego is purifying and is a fit, joyous offering to the Lord.
9. The action, itself, does not purify, but the Knowledge-essence, which discerns the all-importance of God and the utter unimportance of the ego, clears the mind of attachment to the external so that an inquiry that reveals the Truth of the Self commences to shine.
10. Offering is characterized by the relinquishment of "I" and "mine" and Liberation by their nonexistence.

कायवाङ्मनः कार्यमुत्तमम् ।
पूजनं जपश्चिन्तनं क्रमात् ॥ ४ ॥

kāyavāṅmanaḥ kāryamuttamam ।
pūjanaṁ japaścintanaṁ kramāt ।। 4 ।।

To be done with the body, speech, and mind,
Worship, japa, and contemplation are superior in that succession. (4)

Note: "to be done" can be translated as to be practiced.
"with" is implied.
"worship" is puja.
"japa" is repetition of a mantra.
"contemplation" can be translated as reflection, thinking.
"that" is implied.
"succession" can be translated as proceeding, order.
"in that succession" can be translated as because of the order.
The word for "superior" appears in the first line of the Sanskrit text and can be interpreted as pertaining to "the body, speech, and mind," as well as to their respective practices.

Thus:

1. Superiority rests in being subtler, more interior, vaster, less objective, and its fruit being more enduring and comprehensive.
2. Self-Knowledge is formless, subtlest, innermost, the vastest and the vastness, completely nonobjective, endures forever, and is all-comprehensive.
3. The depth of Knowledge that shines in a spiritual practice determines the depth and fruitfulness of that practice. A practice divested of the Knowledge-essence becomes hollow and inert.
4. The subtler and more interior the instrument utilized, the more extensive the vessel it is and the greater the degree the spiritual Knowledge shines therein.
5. The superiority lies not so much in the manifested activity in which the instruments engage as in the identity of the one who engages them in this manner.
6. The Knowledge does not depend on the instruments or their activity, but they depend on Knowledge, which is Consciousness.

7. True Knowledge does not prohibit the practices but illumines them, guides them, is the power in them, is their aim, and transcends them.
8. The one who knows the body, speech, and mind is not the body, speech, and mind and is not reached or known by the body, speech, and mind. That one is the heart of the worshipper and is that to be worshiped, is the source of the mantra and lends its continuity to the japa, and is the inconceivable essence of the contemplator to be contemplated.
9. Because the nature of the one who strives by practice is the Self, succession to finer practice, which is succession by dissolution of imagined limitations superimposed on the essential Knowledge, is natural.
10. The succession concludes in the homogeneous, infinite Knowledge of the Self, which is the Supreme, beyond which there is nothing else or the possibility of anything else, and which is the self-luminous, ever-existent, one Reality.

जगत ईशधीयुक्तसेवनम् ।
अष्टमूर्तिभृद्देवपूजनम् ॥ ५ ॥

jagata īśadhīyuktasevanam |
aṣṭamūrtibhṛddevapūjanam || 5 ||

Worship united with the understanding that the universe is the Lord
Is worship of God bearing eight forms. (5)

Service of the world united with the understanding of God
Is worship of God bearing eight forms. (5)

Worship with the mind united with the Lord of the universe

Is worship of God bearing eight forms. (5)

Note: "the universe" in the first translation is literally of the universe.
The word for "worship" in the first line also means service.
In the Tamil version, the first line states only "worshiping" according to Sri Sadhu Om and Michael James.
The word for understanding can also mean mind, meditation, spiritual thought.
"bearing" can be translated as wearing.
The eight forms are the earth, water, fire, air, space, the sun, the moon, and humankind.

Thus:

1. The universe is only God perceived as such.
2. The Lord of the universe, who is its sole power, is that very God, who is its sole existence.
3. Boundless spiritual love for the entirety of the universe rests in the mind that is united with God.
4. Union is found in the Knowledge that understands the truth of non-differentiation in which there are no such distinct entities as the world, the individual or mind, and the Supreme or God.
5. Worship is not for acquisition of something in the world, for the world is already the Lord's, but only for the Realization of God, who wears this mere universe and apart from Whom it cannot appear.
6. Understanding God and meditation upon God leave no scope for the ego in this world.
7. Divinely inspired activity performed with this comprehension is service, and the mind's union with God is worship.
8. The Lord of the universe is the Lord of the mind, so "my Lord is the glorious Lord of the universe, my Guru is the glorious Guru of the universe, and my Self is the Self of all beings."

9. The Lord who bears the elements and such forms experienced, the mind as the instrument of experience, and the individualized experiencers are of one nature. That of which all are composed, being the Light of all lights, is Siva, and it is Siva who is worshiped in the mind's union with Him and by serving beings with the knowledge that all are only He.
10. God has no other and wears Himself, and that is service in which this knowledge is certain, and that is worship in which God alone is, with the mind absorbed therein.

उत्तमस्तवादुच्चमन्दतः ।
चित्तजं जपध्यानमुत्तमम् ॥ ६ ॥

uttamastavāduccamandataḥ |
cittajaṁ japadhyānamuttamam || 6 ||

Superior to hymns of praise is loud or soft japa;
Mind-born japa-meditation is the best. (6)

Than the best hymns of praise, loud or soft,
Mind-born japa or meditation is better. (6)

Note: "Superior to hymns of praise" can also be translated as better than excellent praise, in which "better" is to be inferred.
"loud" can be translated as intense.
"or" in the first line is implied.
"soft" can be translated as gentle, slow.
"japa" in the first line is implied.
"Mind-born" can be translated as mental. Cittajam, mind-born, also means love or heart-born.
"or" in the second line is implied.

Thus:

1. The subtler and more interior the orientation, the higher it is, because of the interiorness and formlessness regarded as one's identity.
2. That which is regarded as the identity determines the means utilized to experience the Supreme Self.
3. The efficacy of any means or practice is found in the Knowledge-essence that shines within that context, though the Knowledge, itself, does not depend on such.
4. The essential Knowledge is of the Self. So, the more the identity is that, which is the less misidentification, the better, because wiser, the state, practice, and such are.
5. Distance from the Supreme Self is an illusion due to misidentification. Proximity is due to the dissolution of misidentification. Identity is the utter extinction of misidentification.
6. Seek the source. The end of the practice is the source of it, as well as the means. Knowledge of and abidance as the source, which is the end, which is the means, are the aim. The undivided source of the mantra is Brahman, the Guru, the Self.
7. The subtler, more interior, and less objective is the practice, and the less misidentification is involved, the more continuous it is. Truly, Knowledge is innately continuous, being of the nature of Existence, and ignorance, being unreal, is sporadic and discontinuous even in its imagined appearance.
8. The gross is absorbed in the subtle, and the subtle in the formless. So, sound in the mind and the mind in the Silence of the Self are absorbed.
9. Likewise are the objects in the sensations, the sensations in thought, and thought in Consciousness, which is Being. Consciousness is the self-luminous illuminator of all. The closer the abidance to that, even in and as that, the higher, for there are less or no veils of delusion.
10. He is the singer and the One praised. His Silence is louder than the loudest and softer than the softest, faster than the fastest, slower than the slowest, the intensity and the gentleness, and He it is who activates the mind. His is the

practiced, and He is the unpracticed. He is the return to Himself, the Being of the one who returns, and That to which all return, though He never leaves Himself. The basis of all, the Light of all, He is transcendent of all, in which all ever are.

आज्यधारया स्रोतसा समम् ।
सरलचिन्तनं विरलतः परम् ॥ ७ ॥

ājyadhārayā srotasā samam |
saralacintanaṁ viralataḥ param || 7 ||

Like a stream of ghee or the even current of a river,
Continuous contemplation is superior to that which is intermittent. (7)

Note: "stream" can be translated as flow, current.
"or" is implied.
"even" can be translated as smooth, equivalent.
The first line can be translated as:

By a ghee-stream or by a smooth river current,

"continuous" can be translated as correct, straight, sincere.
"contemplation" can be translated as reflection.
"superior to" can be translated as better than, beyond.
"intermittent" can be translated as interrupted, with interstices, sparse.

Thus:

1. Continuity is of the nature of the Self. Being always is; Consciousness always shines.

2. True Knowledge is of the Self and is continuous. No mental mode is eternal or continuous. Knowledge transcends mental modes.
3. Mental contemplation is discontinuous. Mind-transcendent meditation is naturally continuous.
4. The real is continuous, being ever-existent, and the unreal is discontinuous and not at all existent. Sincere contemplation of the real by the light of the real is unbroken for the discerning Knowledge is, by nature, the ever-existent Consciousness, correct because it is of the true by the true, and straight because of the absence of divisions and dualism.
5. The liquid motion of continuous introspection pours itself until emptied as an offering to Siva, Absolute Being-Consciousness, and flows irresistibly without break, so that the current reaches the ocean of That in which individuality is forever lost. Such is the truth of devotion, also.
6. Interstices are appearances of superimposed delusion and not gaps in the essential Knowledge of Being. Only from the perspective of ignorance is the Knowledge considered discontinuous. Likewise is it with steadiness. From Knowledge, there is neither break nor ignorance.
7. Only from the perspective of the non-Self is there the imagination of another different from the Self, inclusive of the one to so imagine. Only from the unreal does the Reality seem partially real and not entirely so. Ignorance is false, the non-Self is not true and not I, and the unreal does not exist at all. Unreal ignorance cannot alter the immutable Reality of the Self.
8. Continuity of contemplation, even with thought, is better than such disrupted by the pursuit of ignorance in the mind and derives its evenness, freedom, and joy proportionately from the Knowledge-essence. Knowledge, itself, being of the nature of Consciousness, is entirely beyond thought and the possibility of interruption.
9. Knowledge of the source of happiness draws one to it continuously, because of its Bliss. Sparseness and interruptions of spiritual practice are due to not understand-

ing this. Continuous joy is natural, as Being is ever existent and ever perfectly full.

10. The continuous, by means of the continuous, drawn by the continuous, reaches the continuous, and the continuous alone remains.

भेदभावनात्सोऽहमित्यसौ ।
भावनाऽभिदा पावनी मता ॥ ८ ॥

bhedabhāvanātso'hamityasau |
bhāvanā'bhidā pāvanī matā || 8 ||

Better than a conception of difference is that "I am He," thus.
Meditation without difference is considered holy. (8)

Note: "Better" is implied.
The same word for "conception" in the first line is translated as "meditation" in the second line. In the first line, it can be translated as conception, meditation, or imagination.
"of difference" can be translated as with differentiation.
Therefore, the first phrase of the first line can be translated as Better than meditation with differentiation.
"I am He" is literally He I am.
"without difference" can be translated as without split, without separation.
"holy" can be translated as purifying.
In the Tamil version, the meaning in line two is, "is preferable" according to B. V. Narasimhaswami.

Thus:

1. Nonduality is Truth. Differentiation is imagination.
2. To include the ignorant conception that creates the illusory bondage, the imagination of differentiation, in the means applied for the attainment of the liberating Knowledge of the difference-less Self, is unwise.
3. The profound Knowledge of the true nature of the meditator is deep, nondual meditation; thus, the inquiry into the identity of the inquirer. This is wise.
4. Difference is delusion. Difference-and-non-difference is confusion with some clarity. No-difference is true Knowledge.
5. As Knowledge is said to destroy ignorance, difference-less meditation is said to purify one of illusory separation from the Supreme Self.
6. The Supreme Self is the holiest of the holiest—beyond comparison at all—because it is absolutely One, eternal, and of the nature of ever-gracious Bliss. Absence of the ego and its concomitant illusory differentiation is sacred abidance in That, as That, itself.
7. "He" is Siva, of the nature of absolute Being-Consciousness-Bliss, also known as Brahman, described as the True-the Knowledge-the Infinite, and realized as the Supreme Self, the one Reality, free of objective conception and creation.
8. "I" am the Self, which is oneself, of the nature of perpetual, immutable, beginningless and endless Existence, nonobjective, indivisible Consciousness, and uncaused, innate Bliss, bodiless, mind-free, egoless, free of misidentification, and unborn.
9. "Am" is the identity of That, Siva, and one's only Self. "Am" is the quintessential Knowledge, in which Being is the Knowledge. It is differenceless.
10. The supremely holy, nondual Being-Knowledge is transcendent of any thought about it and characterized by the absence of the assumed individuality of a knower.

भावशून्यसद्भावसुस्थितिः ।
भावनाबलाद्भक्तिरुत्तमा ॥ ९ ॥

bhāvaśūnyasadbhāvasusthitiḥ ।
bhāvanābalādbhaktiruttamā ।। 9 ।।

Devoid of bhava is being well-established in true Existence.
From the strength of meditation is the supreme devotion. (9)

Note: "bhava" (bhāva) means conception, thought, supposition, state, becoming, world.
"true Existence" can be translated as true Being.
"is being well-established in true Existence" can be translated as is the well-being of true Being, or as is the excellent position of Real Being.
"the supreme" can be translated as the highest.

Thus:

1. Existence ever exists and is never more or less. It is devoid of "other." Nonexistence does not exist or is only Existence.
2. The world and such are a state of becoming, which is only a supposition conceived in thought.
3. The blissful well-being of true Being rests upon its freedom from conception and supposition.
4. As there are not two selves, so that one should be established in the other, being well-established signifies the true Existence free of obscuring concepts or suppositions.
5. Spiritual strength lies in the truth of the Self's Being, how real Reality is, and is akin to finding how existent Existence is.
6. Therefore, strength of meditation is determined by being devoid of ignorance. The strength of Knowledge is the

impotence of ignorance, the steadiness of Knowledge is the unsteadiness of ignorance, and the realization of the real Self is the un-realizing of the unreal, which is the discernment of just how unreal the unreal really is.

7. Devotion is dependence on God, adherence to God, dissolution in God, and abidance as God. God is thought-transcendent, as the Self is, and as Knowledge of the Self is, so is devotion.
8. Depth of Knowledge and height of devotion are the same. The Supreme Knowledge is the Supreme Devotion, and that is free of any difference, of the assumed individual and the supposed world.
9. The strength of meditation, the conviction in the Truth of Being, Siva, brings forth and shines as the certainty of Knowledge and the highest devotion beyond all modes of the mind.
10. He who is the true Existence reveals himself, the true Existence. Abidance as only that Existence is profound meditation upon the revealed and supreme devotion to Him.

हृत्स्थले मनः स्वस्थता क्रिया ।
भक्तियोगबोधाश्च निश्चितम् ॥ १० ॥

hṛtsthale manaḥ svasthatā kriyā |
bhaktiyogabodhāśca niścitam || 10 ||

The mind in the place of the Heart is Self-abidance;
This is certainly action, devotion, yoga, and Knowledge. (10)

Note: "place" can be translated as ground. "Self-abidance" can be translated as being the

Self, being in one's own natural state, being at ease.
"This is" is implied.
"action" can be translated as purificatory action, ritual.
"yoga" can be translated as union.
"certainly" can be translated as it is ascertained.
The Tamil text begins this verse with, "Absorption in the source," according to B. V. Narasimhaswami.

Thus:

1. The Heart is quintessential Being in which difference is impossible. Whatever is in that does not retain individuality.
2. As Being is Consciousness, it knows itself. No other exists to do so. The mind seems to be a supposed individual knower who is second to the second-less Consciousness.
3. With the mind in the Heart, the Self abides as itself, for it alone can be itself. This is one's natural state, full of bliss and peace.
4. The Knowledge that the mind has no separate existence is its "destruction" and the destruction of its forms or manifestations, too, such as ignorance, its effect of bondage, and the consequent suffering. Abidance as the Self is liberation from all of these.
5. Ritual is to worship the unmanifested by means of the manifested, purificatory action is to remove the stain of delusion, and action is to accomplish. The mind in the Heart is the highest, worshipful ritual, and, destroying the illusion of darkness to reveal the ever-stainless Self, such Self-abidance is that which is to be accomplished and the activity that does so.
6. Devotion is to give oneself up to the Absolute, which is Supreme Being, and is love of God for the sake of God alone. Abidance as the Self, in which there is no mind to imagine distinctions, which is the utter effacement of the

ego, worshiping God without another, and loving God as the Self, is the essential devotion.

7. Yoga is union with That and the means thereto. The mind in the Heart is the disappearance of its illusory separation from That and the cessation of the belief in thought as existent. Self-abidance, the Realization of the eternally indivisible true nature, is the great yoga, the Oneness of which can never be fractured.
8. Knowledge is wisdom transcendent of notions, the ascertainment of Reality just as it is. Self-abidance is Self-Knowledge, Reality comprehending itself, self-illumined, in which that which is to be known, the knowledge, and the knower are identical—the undivided Consciousness, indivisible Being.
9. The ability to know belongs to Consciousness alone. One's Existence is certain, the Knowledge of Existence is certain, and the Consciousness that knows that, which is the Existence, is certain. Where there is duality, as it were, there is scope for doubt, but for that which is non-dual, there is this doubtless certainty.
10. The wise ascertain with certitude the nature of Truth by Self-Knowledge. What they know they are. At ease in the Self, they are a Light for which darkness cannot be, and from this, by Grace, pours forth the teaching that reveals all.

वायुरोधनाल्लीयते मनः ।
जालपक्षिवद्रोधसाधनम् ॥ ११ ॥

vāyurodhanāllīyate manaḥ |
jālapakṣivadrodhasādhanam || 11 ||

From control of prana, the mind dissolves;
Like a bird in a net, it is a means for control. (11)

Note: The word interpreted as "prana" means breath, air. "Prana" means vital air, life breath, vitality, animating life-energy.

"dissolves" can be translated as disappears, settles, adheres.
"a means" can be translated as a practice.
"control" can be translated as prevention, checking.

Thus:

1. The mind appears as if solidified by adherence to what is conceived within it and thereby becomes unsettled.
2. What is conceived within it is further imagined to be external to it, though that imagination is, also, only within it.
3. By adherence to that which is interior to it or by disentangling it from external attachments, the mind settles, dissolves, and disappears.
4. Prana, the animating life energy, is necessary for the mind to manifest as that portion of itself that appears as the senses. Control of the prana can determine this manifestation.
5. Though an appearance within the mind, as is all that is manifested, prana, in turn, affects the mind. None of this affects the Self.
6. Control of prana is by the mind, and, by this means, the mind can control itself.
7. The control is a result of both the relationship of mind and prana and the concentration employed.
8. The mind's dissolution by this means is proportionate to the abandonment of its consideration of and attachment to that which is external, such as the world, the body, the senses, etc.
9. The bird of the mind is prevented from flying afar in the sky of imagination by the net of this control, yet its tendency to do so is not thereby destroyed. Destruction of ignorance and the unreal is by Knowledge alone.
10. A spiritual practice may be based on that which is objective or that which is nonobjective, upon the perceived experience or the nature of the imperceptible knower, and aimed at the control of thought or understanding the

mind's true nature, at a transient result or the eternal. One assumes an "I," and the other inquires to know the "I." The means employed are different and the result is different.

चित्तवायवश्चित्क्रियायुताः ।
शाखयोर्द्वयी शक्तिमूलका ॥ १२ ॥

cittavāyavaścitkriyāyutāḥ |
śākhayordvayī śaktimūlakā || 12 ||

Mind and prana are Consciousness combined with activity
And are two branches rooted in sakti. (12)

Note: vāyavaḥ literally means relating to wind or air. It is interpreted here as "prana" and could be translated as breaths or prana-s.
"combined with" can be translated as connected to, endowed with.
The first line can be translated as:

Mind and prana are the connections of Consciousness and activity.

The first line can also be translated as:

Mind and prana are combined with (connected to) the activity of Consciousness.

"and are two branches" is literally of two branches or from two branches.
"sakti" means power.
"rooted in sakti" can be translated as of the same source of power. "same" is implied.

Thus:

1. Consciousness is innately unmoving, and, being absolute, is eternally so without any modification ever.
2. If there is motion, it is only the infinite Consciousness that appears as that which moves and its motion within itself.
3. Consciousness combined with the supposition of activity appears as the mind and prana. Such are only the activity of Consciousness.
4. The supposition of the connection of activity with Consciousness depends on the supposition of a connection between Consciousness and the mind and prana.
5. The appearances of mind and prana are rooted in the same power. The power of the mind and prana is of the same root. This one root power, sakti, is never apart from Siva, of the nature of absolute Consciousness.
6. Without prana, there can be no life of the body, senses, and such. Without the mind, there can be no cognition, thought, and such. Without Consciousness, these cannot be or be known. The root of their power, existence, and the knowledge of them is Consciousness.
7. The activity of Consciousness is perceived only by the activity of Consciousness. The existence of the mind is conceived only in the mind, and the mind and prana are perceived only by the mind with prana. Moreover, Consciousness is the only knower.
8. Consciousness is always undifferentiated. Spiritual instruction pertaining to any apparent difference is only for the purpose of revealing the undifferentiated, pertaining to multiplicity to reveal the nondual, pertaining to the unreal to reveal the real, pertaining to the created to reveal the uncreated, and pertaining to the branches to trace, discern, and reveal the root.
9. One who abides in the source is not misidentified with the branches. The nature of that one is solely Consciousness, which alone can abide as itself. Even while the branches are still held aloft, that one abides as the indestructible root and is thus fully liberated while alive.

10. The mind and prana are known by their activity. The Self, Consciousness, is the power that shines as their activity yet remains as their transcendent knower. The Self is the root of all the branches yet remains without branches and is rootless. The Self is never associated with anything else, yet all are ever in union with it.

लयविनाशने उभयरोधने ।
लयगतं पुनर्भवति नो मृतम् ॥ १३ ॥

layavināśane ubhayarodhane |
layagataṁ punarbhavati no mṛtam || 13 ||

Dissolution and utter destruction are both control.
The dissolved again becomes, not the dead. (13)

Note: "are both control" can be translated as are two kinds of control.

Thus:

1. To change the form of ignorance, even stoppage of thinking the thoughts composing it, without Knowledge of the Truth, is merely temporary dissolution.
2. True Knowledge completely destroys ignorance, inclusive of its forms and very existence. When one knows ignorance to be just ignorance, it ceases to exist.
3. A change of the mind's state or mode is changeful. The cessation of the mind, itself, by true Knowledge is forever.
4. A change of the senses and their activities is temporary respite. Knowledge of the one source of happiness is permanent freedom from attachment. Destroyed by blissful Knowledge, ignorance does not revive.
5. A change of state is temporary relief from the forms of the unreal. Knowledge of the Reality, self-revealed in the

comprehension of how unreal the unreal is, is complete destruction of the unreal forever. Destroyed by real Knowledge, ignorance does not revive.

6. A change of thought and even its stoppage, by means of prana or mind, may bring a temporary dissolution of the form of one's identity. Knowledge of the Self completely destroys the misidentifications, the tendency to misidentify, and the "I" that is involved in such. Destroyed by Self-Knowledge, ignorance does not revive.
7. Destruction is only of the unreal. That which is real cannot be destroyed at any time.
8. If believed to exist, the actually unreal, after dissolution, seems to return. That which is destroyed by the Knowledge of Existence does not recur, for how can that which never was be created again?
9. A mind in abeyance is only restrained. Absorption in Self-Knowledge is a mind that has ceased. Outwardly and transiently they may appear similar, yet, inwardly and lastingly, they are entirely distinct.
10. Self-inquiry aims at the death of the mind, in which its content and the very notion of an existent mind are, with finality, abandoned and gone. Finality lies in the absoluteness of the utterly nondual Self.

प्राणबन्धनाल्लीनमानसम् ।
एकचिन्तनान्नाशमेत्यदः ॥ १४ ॥

prāṇabandhanāllīnamānasam |
ekacintanānnāśametyadaḥ || 14 ||

From the binding of the prana, the mind is dissolved.
From one thought, that reaches destruction. (14)

Note: "binding" can be translated as suppressing.
"is dissolved" can be translated as merges.
"From one thought" can be translated as from thinking of the One, from contemplating the One, from a singular contemplation.
"reaches" can be translated as enters into, comes to.
In the Tamil version, instead of "from one thought," the second line begins with the one path or the path of knowing or the path of becoming one, according to Sri Sadhu Om and Michael James.

Thus:

1. Prana does not know. When suppressed or controlled, it does not know it is so. If prana dissolves or merges, it does not know in what it dissolves or with what it merges.
2. The mind does not know. When dissolved or merged, it does not know in what it is dissolved or with what it is merged.
3. The one Consciousness alone knows. The mind is not a second knower. It is merely the known and cannot know true Knowledge.
4. Alteration, reduction, dissolution, etc., of objective appearance, as the prana alters, reduces, and dissolves the activity of the mind, is not final, for it is not absolute. Nonobjective Self-Knowledge alone destroys illusion.
5. Contemplation of the One becomes singular contemplation in which there is no division of contemplator and contemplated.
6. Thought cannot know. It neither knows itself nor other thoughts. It cannot know the Self. In the thought of the One Self, it is the Knowledge-essence that shines.
7. If that which appears as thought turns inward in a singular manner, the mind is destroyed, and only the one Consciousness remains.

8. That which appears as the one thought, which is the thought of the Absolute Self, of the nonobjective and eternal, of that which is thought-transcendent, is, in essence, really not a thought-form at all. The One Self shines for itself.
9. Due to the singular contemplation, from the one thought of the One, the mind is said to then reach destruction. How can the mind reach where it is not? The one, undifferentiated Consciousness reposes in itself, as itself.
10. Singularly inward turned, contemplating the inconceivable, no second knower is found to exist, and the One alone remains.

नष्टमानसोत्कृष्टयोगिनः ।
कृत्यमस्ति किं स्वस्थितिं यतः ॥ १५ ॥

naṣṭamānasotkṛṣṭayoginaḥ |
kṛtyamasti kiṁ svasthitiṁ yataḥ || 15 ||

For the exalted yogi, with mind destroyed,
Is there anything to be done, since his Self-abidance? (15)

For the exalted yogi, with mind destroyed,
Because of his Self-abidance, is there anything to be done? (15)

With mind destroyed, for the exalted yogi,
What is there to be done? For which reason is his Self-abidance. (15)

Note: "exalted" can be translated as excellent.
mānasa, **translated as "mind," means belonging to the mind or in the mind.**

"Self-abidance" can be translated as abidance in his own natural state.
The word translated as "since," "because," and "for which reason" can be translated as of which, as, because of which.

Thus:

1. With mind destroyed, the yogi exists as only mind-free Being-Consciousness. No mind is no individuality. Being-Consciousness exists as itself.
2. The real Self cannot be destroyed. Only the unreal is destructible. The individual mind is ever unreal and does not realize. The yogi is solely identified as the Real Self, which realizes itself. The yogi who knows the Self is the Self always.
3. Exalted above the world, body, mind, and ego, the yogi's very nature is in union, yoga, with the Absolute Self, for the Self is only One. This is excellent, for such is the highest Bliss.
4. As long as there is anything else other than the supremely blissful, eternal Being of the Self, there will be the urge to accomplish to attain happiness, to know what is real, to find oneself. For the exalted yogi, who rests in That, as That, there is nothing else to be accomplished.
5. For something else, either as purpose or doer, something needs to be done. For the natural state of one's own Self, Being itself, how can there be the ideas of the to-be-done and one who does? Does one do anything to exist? Is Existence not eternal but only to begin at a later time? The exalted yogi abides as his own nature.
6. As Being is ever as it is and is nondual, abidance is Knowledge; not knowledge of or by another, but Knowledge identical with Being. Consciousness is Knowledge.
7. Abidance is Being, not becoming another. The Self is Being. Being is not a thing, an activity, or an event.
8. Activity is for the instruments of body, speech, and mind or for the senses or for the sheaths. Free of misidentifi-

cation with any of these, abiding as the Self alone, the yogi truly never does anything.

9. Being something other than the Self, doing and the to-be-done, and, indeed, anything "else" whatsoever are entirely in and of the mind. These are utterly inapplicable, indeed nonexistent, for the exalted yogi whose mind is destroyed and who thus abides as the Self.
10. The destroyer is Siva, the one who remains is Siva, the excellence is Siva, the yogi is Siva, the all-accomplishing is Siva, the ever-attained is Siva, the Self is Siva, the abidance is Siva, and Siva is always Siva. The yogi attains that which leaves nothing further to be attained, experiences the happiness that leaves no other joy to be desired, knows that which leaves nothing else to know, realizes that which leaves nothing else to realize, and abides as that for which there is no other existence.

दृश्यवारितं चित्तमात्मनः ।
चित्त्वदर्शनं तत्त्वदर्शनम् ॥ १६ ॥

dṛśyavāritaṁ cittamātmanaḥ ।
cittvadarśanaṁ tattvadarśanam ।। 16 ।।

The seen warded off, the mind is of the Self.
The revelation of Consciousness is the revelation of the Truth. (16)

The seen warded off, the mind is of the Self,
Is the revelation of Consciousness. This is the revelation of Truth. (16)

Note: "The seen" can be translated as the perceivable, the objective.
"warded off" can be translated as prevented.
"The seen warded off" can be translated as turned away from the seen.

"revelation" can be translated as perception.

"the mind is of the Self" can be translated as the mind itself, though this translation is potentially applicable only in the second interpretation.

In the second interpretation, "this is" is inferred.

In the Tamil version, the equivalent of the first line says: The mind knowing its own form of light, according to Sri Sadhu Om and Michael James or its own effulgent form according to B. V. Narasimhaswami.

Thus:

1. Consciousness plus the supposition of the objective, gross or subtle, appears as a mind. Devoid of the objective, the only thing that remains of the mind is Consciousness, which is the Self.
2. There is no such thing as a nonobjective thought. There is no such thing as a mind without thought. These are merely imagined where there is, in truth, only one tattva (truth, principle).
3. The objective is form, multiple, transitory, limited, the perceived and conceived, not the Self, and unreal. The nonobjective is formless, nondual, eternal, unlimited, neither perceived nor conceived, is the Self, and is the Reality.
4. The objects are only of the mind, the mind is only of the Self, the Self is only unalloyed, absolute Consciousness, and Consciousness, itself, is the Truth.
5. To know the Truth, one should make his vision nonobjective. Consciousness is Truth. Its revelation of itself to itself is nonobjective.
6. The very Consciousness that, appearing as a mind, turns inward to see the Truth, free of delusive objective definitions, is not a mind at all but is of the very nature of the Self.
7. One who perceives Consciousness is Consciousness, for that is the only knower. The Truth revealed and one for

whom the Truth is revealed are the same, for that is the only Being.

8. Warding off or turning away from the objective is by Knowledge and not by objective means. Knowledge is the fruit of inquiry.
9. The revelation of the Consciousness of the Self, in which the objective illusion of the mind does not arise, is the revelation of Truth.
10. The perception of That is the perception of self-luminous Consciousness, of the Self, which is self-revealed when that which is objective is no longer imagined in the mind.

मानसं तु किं मार्गणे कृते ।
नैव मानसं मार्ग आर्जवात् ॥ १७ ॥

mānasaṁ tu kiṁ mārgaṇe kṛte ।
naiva mānasaṁ mārga ārjavāt ।। 17 ।।

What, then, is the mind? Upon seeking,
There is not, indeed, the mind. This is the direct path. (17)

Note: "seeking" can be translated as investigating, searching.
"upon seeking" can be translated as upon having made the searching, on the investigation being made.
"This is" is implied.
"direct" can be translated as straight.

Thus:

1. The unreal appears as if real by non-inquiry. Upon inquiry, it vanishes.
2. Illusion, such as a mind, is only assumption.

3. True Knowledge, which is the essence of the inquiry, is not unreal, for the unreal cannot destroy itself or reveal its own nonexistence.
4. That which knows that the mind is not existent is not the mind and is never nonexistent. It is immutable, beginningless, and endless.
5. If one assumes that appearances are real, from the form of thoughts, a mind is assumed. If one seeks the mind, itself, there is neither form nor thought, and, devoid of assumptions, no such thing as a mind is found to exist. One formless Consciousness exists and is real.
6. That which does not assume the validity of suppositions concerning what is real and what is "I," but discerns clearly, unimpeded by assumptions, is the direct path, for such inquiry to know oneself does not include any of the dualism that one strives to transcend.
7. To assume that the mind exists and is oneself and, maintaining that supposition, attempt to destroy the mind and its delusions is indirect and is an attempt to realize the Truth upon a basis of that which is false. Knowledge is not attained by means of ignorance. In the abandonment of ignorance, Knowledge shines.
8. Comprehension of ignorance as being only ignorance is its end. The realization of the unreality of the mind is known as its complete, final destruction. For that which was never born, never existed, there is no return.
9. If there were a mind, it might divide the Self from oneself. If there is no mind, there is no such separation.
10. By the direct path of Truth, by the light of inquiry, in which imagined divisions are no longer assumed, the Self knows itself with mind-free Knowledge, as the indivisible one Reality. What could be more direct than the one Self as it is?

वृत्तयस्त्वहंवृत्तिमाश्रिताः ।
वृत्तयो मनो विद्ध्यहं मनः ॥ १८ ॥

vṛttayastvahaṁvṛttimāśritāḥ |
vṛttayo mano viddhyahaṁ manaḥ || 18 ||

Modes of the mind, now, are dependent on the "I" mode.
Modes are the mind; know the "I" is the mind. (18)
Note: "of the mind" is implied.
vṛtti means mode or condition of the mind and, thus, by interpretation, a notion or a thought or an activity of the mind. vṛtti can also be translated as mood of the mind.
"the 'I' mode" can be translated as "I" notion.

Thus:

1. The mind appears as states, modes, and thoughts and has no form apart from them.
2. All of them appear for "I," who is defined as the conceiver or experiencer of them. They depend on "I" and are never experienced independent of "I."
3. That which has only a dependent existence and never otherwise does not actually exist as such or is the non-dependent, actual Existence, the substrate, misperceived as such.
4. The self-existent alone is real and is the Self. One should inquire within and thus abide as the Self, which is self-existent Being, self-existent Consciousness, and self-existent Bliss.
5. The entirety of the mind is merely the "I" notion in various guises.
6. Knowledge resolves the mind into "I." Knowledge is not in the mind. If it were, it would not know the resolution. It is beyond the mind and even knows the "I."
7. The Self is untouched by any thought. The Self is "I"-less.
8. Self-Realization is not a mode of mind. It is not reached by thought or by an assumed, illusory "I." The Self's true

Knowledge of itself, which is just Being, itself, is the nature of Realization.

9. When the "I" is obstructed by notions or conditions of the mind, it is only "I" obstructing itself by itself with itself. A mistake mistakenly mistakes itself as some mistake that is mistaken to be otherwise. Imagination imagines itself to be otherwise.
10. Inquiring, "For whom?" is the cessation of imagination, which returns the sense of reality and identity from the mind, which is only thought, to "I," and thence inquiring "Who am I?" reveals the Self as it is, which is the sole-existent Reality.

अहमयं कुतो भवति चिन्वतः ।
अयि पतत्यहं निजविचारणम् ॥ १९ ॥

ahamayaṁ kuto bhavati cinvataḥ |
ayi patatyahaṁ nijavicāraṇam || 19 ||

From where does this "I" come to be? From one who knows,
Oh! the "I" falls. This is Self-inquiry. (19)

Note: "come to be" can be translated as become.
"knows" can be translated as comprehends, is attentive, thus fixes his mind.
"This is" is implied.
"Self-inquiry" can be translated as constant inquiry, one's own inquiry, inquiry into the Innate.

Thus:

1. This "I" does not come from the objects or the sensations conceived as objects, for the belief in objects is for the "I."

2. This "I" does not come from the body, its activities, its parts, or from a location in it, for the body and such are for the "I."
3. This "I" does not come from thoughts, for they are for "I."
4. "I" cannot arise from another and cannot arise for itself, for another is only for "I," and "for itself" presumes its pre-existence.
5. The supposition of a connection between Being-Consciousness and objects, sensations, a body, and a mind and the supposition of the Self as existing in them or because of them or as possessing them as attributes are delusive.
6. "I" can be only from the Self, yet the immutable Self does not give birth to an "I" at all at any time.
7. The nature of the knower is the Self, so the "I" falls from him, and his own Being is revealed. Therefore, this Self-inquiry is one's own inquiry.
8. Not being of an "I," not being a mental mode, inquiry is constant, just as Consciousness is.
9. Neither of an "I" nor of anything else, the inquiry is into and of the innate, and the Knowledge thus revealed is innate, as Being is.
10. The clarification of the knowledge of one's Being, in which the falsely assumed individuality ceases, is the essential, nonobjective Self-inquiry that yields Liberation from all of the imagined bondage.

अहमि नाशभाज्यहमहंतया ।
स्फुरति हृत्स्वयं परमपूर्णसत् ॥ २० ॥

ahami nāśabhājyahamahaṁtayā |
sphurati hṛtsvayaṁ paramapūrṇasat || 20 ||

Upon the destruction of the "I," as "I," "I,"
Shines the Heart, by itself, the supreme, perfect fullness of Being. (20)

Note: bhāji means participating in, connected to, resorting to, relating to, in which is conspicuous. So, "Upon the destruction of the 'I'" can be translated as connected with the destruction of the "I" or as in which the destruction of the "I" is conspicuous.
"by itself" can be translated as of its own.

Thus:

1. Self-Knowledge born of Self-inquiry that reveals the eternal nonexistence of the ego is the destruction of the "I."
2. Though the Self is fully ever-existent and ever-shining, the belief in an ego, the misidentification as an "I," seems to obscure. The cessation of misidentification leaves the Self shining as the unobscured only Being.
3. The obscuration and the one for whom the Self seems to be obscured are the same unreal "I." The destruction of the "I" is the destruction of all ignorance and obscuration forever.
4. I am only I, the eternal, unalloyed Existence. I am ever I, the perpetual Consciousness. In this Realization, the Self is the Knowledge of itself, as surely as Being and Consciousness are the same, as certainly as I am I.
5. The Light of this absolute Knowledge is the luminosity of one's quintessential Being, which is the Heart. It is realized in identity with it, in which there is no "I" to be different from it.
6. The Heart, quintessential Being, knows itself by itself. Another "I," one who is in any way distinct from the undifferentiated Self, cannot know and truly does not exist.
7. As Being is itself ("I," "I"), as Consciousness knows (shines, flashes forth) by itself, so supreme Bliss exists as the innate fullness and perfection of Absolute Being.
8. The absolute, perfect fullness is ever unfractured and undiminished, just as Being is ever undivided and free of any modification. Omnipresent, there is no scope for an ego in that.

9. The ego "I" is that which appears as the unreal in the midst of the sole-existent Reality, as an individual in the egoless Self, as the veil of the darkness of ignorance for the self-effulgent, infinite Consciousness, and as suffering in the midst of Bliss. The "I" is misidentification, which composes ignorance, which alone is the cause of suffering. The destruction of the "I" notion is the end of all suffering.
10. The supreme, perfect fullness of Being is ever so. This is the Truth. When the "I" is removed from "I," all that remains is the true "I," which is the perfect fullness.

इदमहंपदाभिख्यमन्वहम् ।
अहमिलीनकेऽप्यलयसत्तया ॥ २१ ॥

idamahampadābhikhyamanvaham |
ahamilīnake'pyalayasattayā || 21 ||

This is viewed as the word "I;" every day,
Even upon the dissolution of "I," it is undissolved as Being. (21)

This is viewed as the "I" portion; every day,
Even upon the dissolution of "I," it is undissolved as Being. (21)

The first line may also be translated as:

This is viewed as the word "I" following (along with) "I."

This is viewed as the "I" portion following (along with) "I."

This "I" word is viewed according to "I."

This "I" portion is viewed according to "I."

The second line may also be translated as:

Upon the dissolution of the "I," though, the undissolved Being is.

Upon the dissolution of the "I," though, it is undissolved Being by nature.

Upon the dissolution of the "I," though, it is undissolved on account of Existence.

Note: "viewed as" can be translated as called by.
The word for "word" and "portion" also means abode, characteristic, state.
anvaham, **"every day," can also be interpreted as** anu-aham, **following I, along with I, according to I.**
"Upon the dissolution" can be translated as in dissolution.
"dissolution" can be translated as merger.
ahami-līna-ke'pi **means upon "I" dissolution whatsoever.**
"Being" can be translated as Existence.
According to all of the English translations of the Tamil text, in reference to "everyday," the Tamil version says, "even in sleep."

Thus:

1. This perfectly full Being is to be viewed as truly I. It is this perfectly full Being that is erroneously conceived as an individual "I."
2. The "I" dissolves in deep sleep every day, yet Being remains. Therefore, as one always exists and existence cannot cease to exist, I am not "I" but only indissoluble Being.

3. Being, which never ceases, alone is the abode of "I," and there is no other place for an "I" to be. Being has only itself within it. By this Knowledge of Reality, the supposed "I" portion merges with the undivided, perfectly full, true Being.
4. The significance of the word "I" is according to the identity either conceived as oneself or known as the one Self. Upon the dissolution of the "I" notion, indestructible Existence is realized as its only true meaning.
5. As in the case of "this," the existence of an "I" is only according to the "I." In its true nature, the Being of the Self is devoid of a "this" and of an "I." Only according to the non-Self does the non-Self exist; only according to the unreal does the unreal exist. The belief in and adherence to the "I" follows the assumption of "I." For the Self, the Self alone is; for Reality, there is only Reality.
6. Being can never cease to be. Indissolubility is the very nature of Existence. That which dissolves is not Being and does not really exist.
7. As the dissolution of the unreal does not represent the loss of any real thing and as the Realization of the ever-existent Reality is not the acquisition of anything new, the simultaneous dissolution and Realization are purely of the nature of Self-Knowledge.
8. The various states of creation and dissolution, such as waking, dream, and deep sleep, pertain only to an "I" conceived as other than the Self. The Self is "I"-less, state-less, and free of creation and dissolution.
9. Being is Consciousness and can never be inert or cease to be. Self-Knowledge is of the very nature of this Consciousness and is not contained within or bound by the three states. Self-Knowledge is not for the "I" and is not a state. The permanent dissolution of "I" by keen inquiry is its revelation. Self-Knowledge, being of the nature of Being, itself, is never lost.
10. If one would inwardly inquire so as to cease to misidentify with all that is perishable, or that can dissolve, this would suffice for the Knowledge of the eternal Self.

विग्रहेन्द्रियप्राणधीतमः ।
नाहमेकसत्तज्जडं ह्यसत् ॥ २२ ॥

vigrahendriyaprāṇadhītamaḥ |
nāhamekasattajjaḍaṁ hyasat || 22 ||

The body, the senses, the prana, the intellect and ignorance
Are not I, the one Being. That is inert, for it is unreal. (22)

Note: "intellect" can also be translated as intelligence.
"ignorance" can be translated as darkness.
"Being" can be translated as Existence.
"for" can be translated as indeed.
"it is" is implied.
"unreal" can be translated as nonexistent.
The entire collection of the body, etc., is treated as a single unreality, tat "that."

Thus:

1. The body, subject to birth and death, constituted of parts, changeful, objective, inert in itself, and sporadically experienced, is not the unborn, imperishable, undivided, partless, changeless, nonobjective, continuous Being-Consciousness. It is not I. The one Being alone am I.
2. The senses, subject to appearance and disappearance, multiple, changeful, objective, known by the mind in a particular state of mind, inert and unknown to themselves, and sporadically experienced, are not the non-appearing yet never vanishing, singular and undivided, changeless, nonobjective, unknown by the mind and transcendent of all states of mind, unsensed and self-luminous, continuous Being-Consciousness. They are not I. The one Being alone am I.

3. The prana, subject to coalescence and dispersion, entrance and exit, of various types and conditions, active in various ways, objective, not knowing itself, and non-eternal, is not the space-like, neither entering nor exiting, unconditioned and not multifarious, invariable and ever-unmoving, nonobjective, self-known, and eternal Being-Consciousness. It is not I. The one Being alone am I.
4. The intellect, which appears and disappears, the form of which is thought, which is objective, which is not known by itself, which is not eternal, and which is changeful, is not the non-appearing yet never disappearing, formless, thought-transcendent, nonobjective, self-known, eternal, ever-changeless Being-Consciousness. It is not I. The one Being alone am I.
5. Ignorance, which is as if darkness could be in light, which is imagined and gives rise to the imaginary, which is not eternal, the cause for all differentiation, which does not know itself, and which is not self-existent, is not the ever-shining, self-luminous, real and not imagined, eternal, causeless and without effect, undifferentiated, self-known and self-existent Being-Consciousness. It is not I. The one Being alone am I.
6. I am only the one Existence. There is no other existence, and there is no other "I."
7. The one Being alone is real and alone exists. The unreal is ever nonexistent. There are no degrees of reality. Degrees of unreality are as unreal as the nonexistent, itself.
8. Consciousness alone exists. The inert is truly unreal. All, from ignorance to the body, not being self-known, are not self-existent. They are unreal. The self-existent and self-known is alone real. Therefore, know the knower.
9. The Knowledge of not being the body, senses, prana, the intellect, and ignorance is not for the body, senses, prana, the intellect, and ignorance. They are inert and unreal. The Knowledge is for the Self, which is truly I, which is real, and which is Knowledge itself.
10. Inquiry that negates all misidentification reveals the true identity of ineffable Being, which can neither be conceived nor negated.

सत्त्वभासिका चित्क्ववेतरा ।
सत्तया हि चिच्चित्तया ह्यहम् ॥ २३ ॥

sattvabhāsikā citkvavetarā |
sattayā hi ciccittayā hyaham || 23 ||

The illuminator of Existence is Consciousness. Where is there another?
As Existence is, indeed, Consciousness, as Consciousness, indeed, is "I." (23)

Note: The second line can be translated as:

Existence, by nature, is indeed Consciousness. Consciousness, by nature, is indeed "I."

Thus:

1. The Self is Being-Consciousness. Than Being, there is no other existence. Than Consciousness, there is no other knower or illuminator.
2. Being-Consciousness cannot be known by or through anything other than itself, for the nonexistent cannot realize, and the known cannot know.
3. Self-Knowledge is that in which the Self is the knower, the known, and the knowing and which is of the nature of indivisible Consciousness. Consciousness is the Knowledge.
4. Existence is I. Consciousness is I. I always exist. I always know this Existence.
5. I am. I know that I am. The Knowledge that I am is inseparable from the Existence that I am.
6. Never is there a doubt about Existence. Even if such a doubt could be conjured up, I would exist to know the nonexistence.
7. Consciousness ever shines; I always know. Even if there were the idea of not knowing or being bereft of

Consciousness, that would still be illumined by Consciousness; I would still know.

8. As Being is Consciousness, there is no other to know. Consciousness being "I," there is simply no other.
9. I do not become Consciousness. By my nature, I am Consciousness, and there is no other "I." I do not become Being. By nature, I am Being, and there is no other "I." Self-Knowledge reveals this.
10. The essential teaching is true Knowledge. True Knowledge is Consciousness as it is. "As it is" is just Being. Just Being is the Truth of "I."

ईशजीवयोर्वेषधीभिदा ।
सत्स्वभावतो वस्तु केवलम् ॥ २४ ॥

īśajīvayorveṣadhībhidā ।
satsvabhāvato vastu kevalam ।। 24 ।।

Of both the Lord and the individual, the assumed appearance and intelligence are the difference.
Being's own Existence is the Reality that alone is. (24)

Of both the Lord and the individual, activity and intelligence are the distinction.
The true own Existence is the Reality that alone is. (24)

Of both the Lord and the individual, the thought of the assumed appearance is the difference.
Being's own Existence is the Reality that alone is. (24)

Note: "difference" and "distinction" can be translated as separation.
In the Tamil version, the phrase that pertains to difference translates as, "Adjunct knowledge

alone is different," according to Sri Sadhu Om and Michael James.

Thus:

1. The separation between the Lord and the individual consists of the assumed difference. Real Being is undifferentiated and is ever undivided.
2. Difference is conceived by the individual, who is, himself, an assumed difference. How can he assume himself? Who can say what the inconceivable Lord sees?
3. Difference is only the thought of such. Thought of such does not make it so. The true Existence is free from thought and undefined by thought.
4. It is the Reality of Being, which alone is, that is imagined as differentiated. Once the assumed differentiated appearance is considered real, there is misidentification as an individual of obviously limited intelligence and activity, while the rest of the truly undifferentiated Being is present as the Supreme Lord of inconceivably infinite intelligence and activity.
5. If the assumption of individuality is abandoned, one's undifferentiated real Being is realized to alone exist, and that transcends even the definition or difference of "Lord."
6. The individual does not cease to misidentify; the individual is not real. Cessation of misidentification is abidance as the Existence of the Self, which alone is.
7. If I am the mind and body, I think and act, and so does God in a much vaster way. If I, being bodiless and without a mind, never think or act, likewise is God. Then, I am Being alone, and God is ever only I.
8. Intelligence and activity may be limited, but not so the essential Existence, which is the core Being and substrate of all jiva-s (living beings). What is this essential Existence? The same is even the core and substrate of the Lord of all that is manifested. Appearing as the core and substrate in consideration of the Lord, the individual, and all, the true Existence, which exists by itself, being self-existent, is alone the Reality.

9. The superimposition of illusory attributes upon Being, which is truly the Self, is delusion. Freedom from such misidentification is true Knowledge, revealed by deep inquiry. That which is thus revealed is innate.
10. According to the definitions attributed to "I," the Lord appears. When, in the light of the essential teaching, the definitions are abandoned, and even "I" is not conceived, how is the Lord known? Real Being alone remains, the only Existence in the "I" and the Lord, and That alone has truly ever existed.

वेषहानतः स्वात्मदर्शनम् ।
ईशदर्शनं स्वात्मरूपतः ॥ २५ ॥

veṣahānataḥ svātmadarśanam |
īśadarśanaṁ svātmarūpataḥ || 25 ||

The abandonment of the assumed appearance is the revelation of one's own Self.
The revelation of the Lord is the state of the nature of one's own Self. (25)

Note: "abandonment" can be translated as relinquishment.
"revelation" can be translated as perception.
"one's own" can be translated as the true.

Thus:

1. Assumed appearances are only ignorance, composed of imagination.
2. Abandonment of ignorance, or false appearance, is disbelief in it. When ignorance is known as ignorance, it ceases to exist or appear.
3. The relinquishment of false appearance, the activity of delusion, is not by activity but by Knowledge.

4. The root of ignorance is the one who can be ignorant, and its effect is differentiation. If the Self is known as it is, the ignorant one is not to be found and, likewise, the ignorance.
5. True Knowledge simply reveals. The Self is not obtained or transformed. Its ever-existent true nature remains unobscured by imagination.
6. The Self never has the experience of false appearance. For whom is it? Such inquiry destroys the false appearance and the assumption of one who experiences it.
7. If the Self is not known, God remains a mystery or is conceived in a manner that corresponds to the view of oneself. If the Self, which alone is oneself, is realized as it is, the nature of God is realized to be the same.
8. The Self alone knows the Self. There is no other to do so. God alone knows God. There is no other to do so. In Self-Knowledge, God knows God with God's own eye.
9. The state of one's own nature, the Self, is ever the same. The ever-the-same is immutable, and the immutable is imperishable. The imperishable is eternal. The eternal is the formless Absolute. That is God, who is the Self.
10. The Lord reveals Himself. The Guru reveals his own Existence. The Self reveals itself. The revelation is by their own gracious Light. To whom is it revealed? God, Guru, and the Self are one and the same.

आत्मसंस्थितिः स्वात्मदर्शनम् ।
आत्मनिर्द्वयादात्मनिष्ठता ॥ २६ ॥

ātmasaṁsthitiḥ svātmadarśanam |
ātmanirdvayādātmaniṣṭhatā || 26 ||

Complete abidance as the Self is the revelation of one's own Self.
Because there are not two of the Self, there is firm Self-Abidance. (26)

Note: "revelation" can be translated as perception.
"one's own" can be translated as the true.
"there is" is implied.
The second line can be translated as:

Because there are not two kinds of Self, there is firm Self-abidance.

Thus:

1. The revelation of the Self, which is truly oneself, is nonobjective.
2. The revealed Knowledge is not divided into a knower and a known.
3. Being is Knowledge. It transcends the notions of an event, an experience, a mode, a state, and such.
4. In abidance as the Self, there are not two selves, that one would abide in another. One Self exists.
5. If there is duality, such as the Self and oneself, there is wavering. If the Self is only one, Knowledge is absolutely steady, for one's very Being is the Knowledge.
6. Being, the Self, is without an alternative or another. This is nonduality.
7. If Self-Knowledge were objective, it could be lost. As it is Being, itself, it is ever existent, ever the same, and ever full, just as Being is. There is no second self for whom it could be otherwise.
8. Since the Self is ever as it is, ever the Self, abidance is Knowledge that is identical with Being, free of misidentifications.
9. Because of the nondual nature of Self-abidance, or Self-Realization, the Realization is of the very same nature as the Self, itself. So, all that is the truth regarding the Self is the truth regarding its Realization, or firm Self-abidance.
10. Completeness of abidance rests in the eternal nonexistence of an ego-self.

ज्ञानवर्जिताऽज्ञानहीनचित् ।
ज्ञानमस्ति किं ज्ञातुमन्तरम् ॥ २७ ॥

jñānavarjitā'jñānahīnacit I
jñānamasti kiṁ jñātumantaram II 27 II

Knowledge abandoned, ignorance abandoned, Consciousness is.
Is there knowledge to know difference? (27)

Knowledge abandoned, ignorance abandoned, Consciousness
Is Knowledge. Is there another to know? (27)

Knowledge excluded, ignorance excluded, Consciousness is
Knowledge. Is there any difference to know? (27)

Note: "abandoned" can be translated as excluded.
"difference" can be translated as another.
The word for "difference" or "another" can also mean interior, intimate, the heart, the supreme soul. So, an interpretation of the second line could be: Is there knowledge to know the interior? The Tamil text does not seem to lend itself to this interpretation.

Thus:

1. "I know this" and "I do not know this" are characteristic of the objective outlook that constitutes illusion.
2. The use of the same false, objectifying mode in an attempt to realize the Self is delusive.
3. Consciousness, infinite and ever-existent, is devoid of the so-called ignorance and the so-called knowledge.

Abandonment of "I" and "this" by profound inquiry yields true Knowledge that transcends "knowledge and ignorance."

4. Consciousness, itself, is the true Knowledge, which is Self-Knowledge.
5. Consciousness knows its undifferentiated Self. There is no other one to know it or to know anything else.
6. Consciousness is the only knower and the only knowledge. So, how could there be an object different from it to be known?
7. If the Self were dual, there could be ignorance of it or knowledge of it. The Self is absolutely one. Who is to be ignorant of or to know what?
8. That, by the light of which all, ignorance and knowledge, are known, should be known by its own light, in its own undifferentiated nature. That, by the light of which one inquires, the very essence of the inquirer, should be known by its own light in its own undifferentiated nature. That is Consciousness. That alone is the Self.
9. If there is a state of ignorance, one naturally aspires for a state of knowledge. If there is no ignorant state, knowledge is not a state. The nondual Consciousness is stateless and is, itself, eternal, innate Knowledge. Who is ignorant? Consciousness cannot be so, and there is no other to be so.
10. The ego absent, Consciousness alone is. Free of the primary difference, how could there be any other?

किं स्वरूपमित्यात्मदर्शने ।
अव्ययाभवापूर्णचित्सुखम् ॥ २८ ॥

kiṁ svarūpamityātmadarśane |
avyayābhavāpūrṇacitsukham || 28 ||

For the sake of clarity, some editions of the Sanskrit text print the second line as:

अव्ययाऽभवाऽऽपूर्णचित्सुखम् ॥

avyayā'bhavā''pūrṇacitsukham ||

"What is the true nature?" thus. Upon the revelation of the Self,
It is immutable, birthless, making perfectly full, Consciousness-Happiness. (28)

"What is one's own nature?" thus. In the perception of the Self,
It is imperishable, non-entity, satiating, Consciousness-Happiness. (28)

Note: "true nature" can be translated as one's own nature.
"upon" can be translated as in.
"revelation" can be translated as perception.
"immutable" can be translated as imperishable.
"birthless" can be translated as non-entity.
"making perfectly full" can be translated as satiating.

Thus:

1. Self-inquiry is the inquiry into one's nature, into the truth of one's Being. The inquiry is free of concern with or conception of "this," such as objects, sensations, or thoughts.
2. As there is no other knower or self, the inquiry is entirely beyond the mind. The inquiry is of the nature of Knowledge.
3. The Self reveals itself to itself by itself.
4. Upon this Self-revelation, which is truly timeless, and in this Self-revelation, which is Absolute Knowledge, the Self exists as it is, just Being. It is not being this or that; it is solely Being.

5. Changeless, the Self is imperishable. Being never ceases to be. The endless must be without a beginning. Unborn, it is not an entity, but Being.
6. That which is Being is Consciousness. That which is Being-Consciousness is Bliss. Happiness, itself, is completely satiating. Happiness is perfectly full of itself.
7. Happy is it to truly inquire. Happy is it to know oneself. Happy is it to exist immutably. Happy is it to be indestructible. Happy is it to not imagine oneself as an individual entity. Happy is the Unborn. The happiness of Consciousness is without limit and without end.
8. Ignorance is suffering. Knowledge is bliss. To regard the non-Self as the Self is suffering. To know the Self as it is is bliss. As the Self ever is itself and the non-Self is never the Self, suffering is needless and devoid of a valid cause. He who truly knows this is always happy.
9. To abide as the Self is pure happiness and the only happiness. All other joys are the reflections of innate happiness associated with something. In itself, it is the perfect fullness. How else is there to be Self-abidance except by the profound inquiry to realize the nature of the Self?
10. As Being is indefinable, Consciousness is inconceivable, so Bliss is inexpressible. The Self shines, delighting in itself, full of the ineffable perfection.

बन्धमुक्त्यतीतं परं सुखम् ।
विन्दतीह जीवस्तु दैविकः ॥ २९ ॥

bandhamuktyatītaṁ paraṁ sukham |
vindatīha jīvastu daivikaḥ || 29 ||

Beyond bondage and liberation, the supreme happiness,
He finds here that the jiva is certainly the Divine. (29)

Beyond bondage and liberation,
The divine living being finds here, then, the Supreme Happiness. (29)

Beyond bondage and liberation is the Absolute Happiness;
The living being finds now, certainly, the Divine. (29)

Note: "the supreme happiness" may be interpreted as the Supreme, Happiness.
"here" may be translated as "now."
"the jiva" means the individual, the life.
"certainly" may be translated as but, then.
"Supreme" may be translated as Absolute.

Thus:

1. The Self is Being and never becomes this or that. It has never become bound, so how is the Self to be liberated again?
2. There is no bound individual and, therefore, no bound state. There is no liberated individual, and no liberated state. Being is as it is, stateless and without any individuality.
3. Liberation is not freedom of an individual, but freedom from the individual. Yet, the Self ever is just as it is, forever free of individuality, and so is neither bound nor liberated.
4. Upon the inquiry, "Who is bound?" the nonexistence of the bound one and his bondage is self-evident, and Liberation is no longer conceived as a state, event, experience, and such, but it is realized as the very nature of the Self.
5. Thus is found the Supreme, which is Siva, which is the Self. It is happiness. It is absolute and so not in relation to anything else, for nothing else actually exists, and the one Self alone is real.

6. The individual is only the Self. There is no other, no second.
7. One who realizes the Self is the Self. He is divine. Thus should one recognize him.
8. Here and now, in this very life, is the Realization of the Absolute Self, which is infinite, timeless, and without life-and-death.
9. This Realization leaves nothing else to be realized. This Knowledge leaves nothing else to be known. This Bliss leaves nothing to be desired. This is absolute happiness. This Self is the Reality. This is the Truth.
10. What pertains to the divine Absolute pertains to me; what does not pertain to the divine Absolute does not pertain to me. Thus should one know the truth of oneself.

अहमपेतकं निजविभानकम् ।
महदिदं तपो रमणवागियम् ॥ ३० ॥

ahamapetakaṁ nijavibhānakam |
mahadidaṁ tapo ramaṇavāgiyam || 30 ||

Free from "I," the innate Light,
This is great tapas; this is the saying of
Ramana. (30)

Free from "I" is the innate Light;
This is great tapas; this is the saying of
Ramana. (30)

Free from "I" is the constant Light;
This is great tapas; this is the saying of
Ramana. (30)

Note: "Free from 'I'" can be translated as "I" gone.
"innate" can be translated as constant.

nija-vibhānakam **can also be interpreted as the Light of the Self, or the Light of one's own Self.**

Tapas (tapaḥ) **is intense meditation or fiery austerity.**

"the saying" can be translated as the spoken word, the speech.

Thus:

1. The innate Light, Consciousness, is innately "I"-less.
2. Constant Knowledge of egoless-ness is the intense practice and the great end.
3. The Self is one's own self. Therefore, there is Self-illumination.
4. Silence has spoken. Such is the word of Ramana.
5. Ramana is the Self. The Self revealed itself. This is the word of Ramana.
6. The power of His word is the power of Brahman, of Siva, for He is That.
7. The One who is delightful gladdens the heart in an unsurpassed way. Seek Him and know Him as He is.
8. Sri Ramana has given His word. Follow it, adhere to it, know it, and abide in its Truth.
9. His word is that which no "I" can survive. His Silence is that in which no "I" can appear.
10. Conclusive Realization of the Truth that He is and reveals is the completeness of the absorption and the knowledge of the essential spiritual instruction of Sri Ramana.

श्री
उपदेशसारः ॥
संपूर्णः ॥

śrī
upadeśasāraḥ ||
sampūrṇaḥ ||

**The Holy
Essence of the Spiritual Instruction
concludes.**

Note: "holy" can be translated as glorious, radiant.
"concludes" can be translated as is complete.

In the Temple of Being,
The Space of Consciousness,

ॐ श्री रमणार्पणमस्तु

om śrī ramaṇārpaṇamastu

Om. May this be an offering to Sri Ramana.

Appendix

॥ श्री उपदेशसारः ॥

|| śrī upadeśa-sāraḥ ||

कर्तुराज्ञया प्राप्यते फलम् ।
कर्म किं परं कर्म तज्जडम् ॥ १ ॥

kartur-ājñayā prāpyate phalam |
karma kiṁ paraṁ karma taj-jaḍam || 1 ||

कृतिमहोदधौ पतनकारणम् ।
फलमशाश्वतं गतिनिरोधकम् ॥ २ ॥

kṛti-mahodadhau patana-kāraṇam |
phalam-aśāśvataṁ gati-nirodhakam || 2 ||

ईश्वरार्पितं नेच्छया कृतम् ।
चित्तशोधकं मुक्तिसाधकम् ॥ ३ ॥

īśvarārpitaṁ necchayā kṛtam |
citta-śodhakaṁ mukti-sādhakam || 3 ||

कायवाङ्मनः कार्यमुत्तमम् ।
पूजनं जपश्चिन्तनं क्रमात् ॥ ४ ॥

kāya-vāṅ-manaḥ kāryam-uttamam |
pūjanaṁ japaś-cintanaṁ kramāt || 4 ||

जगत ईशधीयुक्तसेवनम् ।
अष्टमूर्तिभृद्देवपूजनम् ॥ ५ ॥

jagata īśa-dhī-yukta-sevanam |
aṣṭamūrti-bhṛd-deva-pūjanam || 5 ||

उत्तमस्तवादुच्चमन्दतः ।
चित्तजं जपध्यानमुत्तमम् ॥ ६ ॥

uttama-stavād-ucca-mandataḥ |
cittajaṁ japa-dhyānam-uttamam || 6 ||

आज्यधारया स्रोतसा समम् ।
सरलचिन्तनं विरलतः परम् ॥ ७ ॥

ājya-dhārayā srotasā samam |
sarala-cintanaṁ viralataḥ param || 7 ||

भेदभावनात्सोऽहमित्यसौ ।
भावनाऽभिदा पावनी मता ॥ ८ ॥

bheda-bhāvanāt-so'ham-ityasau |
bhāvanā'bhidā pāvanī matā || 8 ||

भावशून्यसद्भावसुस्थितिः ।
भावनाबलाद्भक्तिरुत्तमा ॥ ९ ॥

bhāva-śūnya-sadbhāva-susthitiḥ |
bhāvanā-balād-bhaktir-uttamā || 9 ||

हृत्स्थले मनः स्वस्थता क्रिया ।
भक्तियोगबोधाश्च निश्चितम् ॥ १० ॥

hṛt-sthale manaḥ svasthatā kriyā |
bhakti-yoga-bodhāśca niścitam || 10 ||

वायुरोधनाल्लीयते मनः ।
जालपक्षिवद्रोधसाधनम् ॥ ११ ॥

vāyu-rodhanāl-līyate manaḥ |
jāla-pakṣivad-rodha-sādhanam || 11 ||

चित्तवायवश्चित्क्रियायुताः ।
शाखयोर्द्वयी शक्तिमूलका ॥ १२ ॥

citta-vāyavaś-cit-kriyāyutāḥ |
śākhayor-dvayī śakti-mūlakā || 12 ||

लयविनाशने उभयरोधने ।
लयगतं पुनर्भवति नो मृतम् ॥ १३ ॥

laya-vināśane ubhaya-rodhane |
laya-gataṁ punar-bhavati no mṛtam || 13 ||

प्राणबन्धनाल्लीनमानसम् ।
एकचिन्तनान्नाशमेत्यदः ॥ १४ ॥

prāṇa-bandhanāl-līna-mānasam |
eka-cintanān-nāśametyadaḥ || 14 ||

नष्टमानसोत्कृष्टयोगिनः ।
कृत्यमस्ति किं स्वस्थितिं यतः ॥ १५ ॥

naṣṭa-mānasotkṛṣṭa-yoginaḥ ।
kṛtyam-asti kiṁ sva-sthitiṁ yataḥ ।। 15 ।।

दृश्यवारितं चित्तमात्मनः ।
चित्त्वदर्शनं तत्त्वदर्शनम् ॥ १६ ॥

dṛśya-vāritaṁ cittam-ātmanaḥ ।
cittva-darśanaṁ tattva-darśanam ।। 16 ।।

मानसं तु किं मार्गणे कृते ।
नैव मानसं मार्ग आर्जवात् ॥ १७ ॥

mānasaṁ tu kiṁ mārgaṇe kṛte ।
naiva mānasaṁ mārga ārjavāt ।। 17 ।।

वृत्तयस्त्वहंवृत्तिमाश्रिताः ।
वृत्तयो मनो विद्ध्यहं मनः ॥ १८ ॥

vṛttayastvahaṁ-vṛttim-āśritāḥ ।
vṛttayo mano viddhyahaṁ manaḥ ।। 18 ।।

अहमयं कुतो भवति चिन्वतः ।
अयि पतत्यहं निजविचारणम् ॥ १९ ॥

aham-ayaṁ kuto bhavati cinvataḥ ।
ayi patatyahaṁ nija-vicāraṇam ।। 19 ।।

अहमि नाशभाज्यहमहंतया ।
स्फुरति हृत्स्वयं परमपूर्णसत् ॥ २० ॥

ahami nāśa-bhājy-aham-ahaṁtayā |
sphurati hṛt-svayaṁ parama-
pūrṇa-sat || 20 ||

इदमहंपदाभिख्यमन्वहम् ।
अहमिलीनकेऽप्यलयसत्तया ॥ २१ ॥

idam-aham-padābhikhyam-anvaham |
ahami-līnake'pyalaya-sattayā || 21 ||

विग्रहेन्द्रियप्राणधीतमः ।
नाहमेकसत्तज्जडं ह्यसत् ॥ २२ ॥

vigrahendriya-prāṇa-dhī-tamaḥ |
nāham-eka-sat-taj-jaḍaṁ hyasat || 22 ||

सत्त्वभासिका चित्क्ववेतरा ।
सत्तया हि चिच्चित्तया ह्यहम् ॥ २३ ॥

sattva-bhāsikā cit-kvavetarā |
sattayā hi cic-cittayā hy-aham || 23 ||

ईशजीवयोर्वेषधीभिदा ।
सत्स्वभावतो वस्तु केवलम् ॥ २४ ॥

īśa-jīvayor-veṣa-dhī-bhidā |
sat-svabhāvato vastu kevalam || 24 ||

वेषहानतः स्वात्मदर्शनम् ।
ईशदर्शनं स्वात्मरूपतः ॥ २५ ॥

veṣa-hānataḥ svātma-darśanam ।
īśa-darśanaṁ svātma-rūpataḥ ।। 25 ।।

आत्मसंस्थितिः स्वात्मदर्शनम् ।
आत्मनिर्द्वयादात्मनिष्ठता ॥ २६ ॥

ātma-saṁsthitiḥ svātma-darśanam ।
ātma-nirdvayād-ātma-niṣṭhatā ।। 26 ।।

ज्ञानवर्जिताऽज्ञानहीनचित् ।
ज्ञानमस्ति किं ज्ञातुमन्तरम् ॥ २७ ॥

jñāna-varjitā'jñāna-hīnacit ।
jñānam-asti kiṁ jñātum-antaram ।। 27 ।।

किं स्वरूपमित्यात्मदर्शने ।
अव्ययाभवापूर्णचित्सुखम् ॥ २८ ॥

kiṁ svarūpam-ityātma-darśane ।
avyayābhavāpūrṇa-cit-sukham ।। 28 ।।

बन्धमुक्त्यतीतं परं सुखम् ।
विन्दतीह जीवस्तु दैविकः ॥ २९ ॥

bandha-muktyatītaṁ paraṁ sukham ।
vindatīha jīvastu daivikaḥ ।। 29 ।।

अहमपेतकं निजविभानकम् ।
महदिदं तपो रमणवागियम् ॥ ३० ॥

aham-apetakaṁ nija-vibhānakam |
mahad-idaṁ tapo ramaṇa-vāg-iyam || 30 ||

ॐ

SAT

SOCIETY OF ABIDANCE IN TRUTH

1834 OCEAN STREET, SANTA CRUZ, CALIFORNIA 95060

(831) 425-7287 ~ www.SATRamana.org ~ sat@cruzio.com